VIRTUAL VENTURES

Exploring Tech Trends in the Real Estate Industry

NELLA BYRAN

Copyright

No part of this should be reproduced without the permission of the author.

© Nella Byran 2024

Contents

Introduction 4

Virtual Reality 7

Augmented Reality Applications: Enhancing Property Marketing and Sales 10

'Interactive Property Tours: Immersive Experiences for Prospective Buyers 14

Virtual Staging 18

Remote Collaboration Tools: Streamlining Communication and Decision Making 22

Blockchain in Real Estate Transactions 26

AI-Powered Property Insights: Leveraging Data Analytics for Informed Decisions 30

Smart Home Integration 34

Digital Marketing Strategies 38

Online Auction Platforms: Modernizing Property Sales Processes 42

Virtual Property Management 46

Remote Work and the Future of Commercial Real Estate 50

Cybersecurity Measures 55

Proptech Investments: Opportunities and Challenges in Tech-Driven Ventures 59

The Next Frontier 63

Conclusion 67

Introduction

Welcome to the frontier of real estate innovation, where traditional bricks-and-mortar meet the boundless possibilities of the digital realm. In "Virtual Ventures: Exploring Tech Trends in the Real Estate Industry," we embark on a journey through the transformative landscape of property exploration, sales, management, and beyond, all driven by cutting-edge technologies.

The convergence of virtual reality (VR), augmented reality (AR), artificial intelligence (AI), blockchain, and more has ushered in a new era of possibilities for stakeholders in the real estate sector. No longer confined by physical limitations, prospective buyers can now immerse themselves in virtual tours of properties, visualizing spaces with unprecedented clarity and detail, thanks to advancements in VR and AR technologies.

But the impact of technology doesn't end with property exploration; it extends to every facet of the real estate lifecycle. From streamlining marketing efforts through interactive tours and virtual staging to enhancing collaboration among stakeholders through remote communication tools, the digital revolution is reshaping how properties are marketed, sold, and managed.

Blockchain technology promises unparalleled transparency, security, and efficiency in real estate transactions, revolutionizing the way properties change hands. Meanwhile, AI-powered analytics provide valuable insights into market trends and buyer preferences, empowering stakeholders to make informed decisions with confidence.

The concept of a "smart home" is no longer confined to the realm of science fiction; it's a tangible reality, with IoT devices and smart systems seamlessly integrated into living spaces, enhancing comfort, convenience, and sustainability.

As we delve deeper into the virtual landscape of real estate, we must also confront the challenges it presents, from cybersecurity threats to the need for ongoing investment and adaptation. Yet, with every challenge comes opportunity, and "Virtual Ventures" explores the myriad opportunities and potential pitfalls of propelling the industry forward into the digital age.

Join us as we navigate this exciting frontier, exploring emerging technologies, innovative strategies, and the limitless possibilities they present for the future of real estate. Whether you're a seasoned industry professional or a curious newcomer, prepare to be inspired, informed, and empowered to embrace the virtual ventures that lie ahead.

Virtual Reality

In the opening chapter of "Virtual Ventures," we plunge headfirst into the captivating world of virtual reality (VR) and its profound impact on the way we explore and visualize real estate properties. Gone are the days of static images and flat floor plans; VR technology offers a dynamic, immersive experience that brings properties to life like never before.

Imagine stepping into a potential new home without ever leaving your living room. With VR headsets, prospective buyers can embark on virtual tours of properties from anywhere in the world, experiencing every room and detail as if they were physically present. From soaring ceilings to sun-drenched windows, VR allows buyers to immerse themselves in the essence of a property, gaining a comprehensive understanding of its layout, design, and ambiance.

However, VR has an impact that goes beyond simple exploring; it completely changes how properties are advertised and presented. Professionals in real estate can now produce engaging, three-dimensional virtual tours that make properties stand out from the competition. Through the utilization of virtual reality technology, real estate brokers can offer potential purchasers an unmatched perception of space and magnitude, cultivating a more profound emotional bond with the asset from the comforts of their own homes.

Moreover, VR isn't just for residential properties; it's also transforming the way commercial real estate is marketed and leased. From office buildings to retail spaces, VR allows tenants to visualize themselves in a prospective space, evaluating layout options and envisioning the possibilities for their businesses.

The benefits of VR in real estate are manifold, offering increased efficiency, reduced costs, and greater accessibility for buyers and sellers alike. For developers and architects, VR provides a powerful tool for showcasing planned projects, allowing stakeholders to visualize the finished product and make informed decisions throughout the design and development process.

As we immerse ourselves in the world of VR in real estate, we'll uncover the latest innovations in technology, from photorealistic rendering to immersive virtual experiences. We'll explore the challenges and opportunities that lie ahead, from ensuring accessibility for all users to navigating the ethical implications of this transformative technology. Whether you're a seasoned real estate professional or a curious enthusiast, prepare to be dazzled by the possibilities of VR and its role in redefining property exploration and visualization. Welcome to the future of real estate—where the impossible becomes possible, and dreams become reality.

Augmented Reality Applications: Enhancing Property Marketing and Sales

Welcome to a world where reality is enhanced, where the line between the physical and the digital blurs to create immersive experiences unlike any other. In this chapter, we dive into the realm of augmented reality (AR) and its profound impact on revolutionizing property marketing and sales.

Imagine holding up your smartphone or tablet and watching as a property comes to life before your eyes. With augmented reality, the static pages of a brochure or the screen of a device become portals into dynamic, interactive experiences. AR overlays digital content onto the real world, allowing prospective buyers to visualize properties in ways that were once unimaginable.

Picture yourself standing outside a charming townhouse, scanning a QR code, and instantly seeing a virtual tour materialize in front of you. With AR technology, prospective buyers can explore every room, from the cozy living area to the spacious master bedroom, all from the palm of their hand. They can interact with virtual furniture, rearranging layouts to suit their tastes, and even envisioning future renovations or decor choices.

But AR isn't just about exploration; it's a powerful tool for driving engagement and generating leads. Real estate professionals can leverage AR applications to create interactive marketing campaigns that captivate audiences and set properties apart from the competition. Whether through interactive property listings or virtual staging experiences, AR allows agents to showcase properties in a way that resonates with buyers on a deeper, more personal level.

Moreover, AR empowers buyers to make more informed decisions by providing valuable contextual information about properties and neighborhoods. With AR-enabled devices, prospective buyers can access real-time data overlays, such as nearby amenities, property history, and market trends, empowering them to make confident, well-informed choices about their investments.

But perhaps most importantly, AR enhances the sales process by breaking down barriers and facilitating communication between buyers and sellers. With AR technology, agents can conduct virtual property tours, host interactive open houses, and even facilitate remote negotiations, bridging the gap between buyers and properties regardless of location or time constraints.

We will examine the most recent technological developments, optimal implementation strategies, and the countless opportunities to improve property marketing and sales as we go deeper into the realm of augmented reality applications in real estate. Prepare to be astounded by the revolutionary potential of augmented reality and its role in influencing the future of the real estate business, whether you're an experienced professional or just a curious enthusiast. Greetings from a new era in real estate sales and marketing, where opportunities abound and reality is enhanced.

'Interactive Property Tours: Immersive Experiences for Prospective Buyers

In the realm of real estate, the traditional model of property viewing has undergone a profound evolution, thanks to the emergence of interactive property tours. These tours represent a groundbreaking shift from static images and floor plans to dynamic, immersive experiences that engage and captivate prospective buyers like never before.

At the heart of interactive property tours lies the concept of immersion. Unlike traditional property listings, which offer only glimpses of a property's potential, interactive tours invite buyers to step into the virtual world of the property, exploring every room and detail with unparalleled depth and clarity. From the grandeur of a sweeping staircase to the tranquility of a sun-drenched patio, interactive tours allow buyers to experience the essence of a property in all its glory.

But what sets interactive tours apart is their interactivity. Unlike pre-recorded video tours, which offer a passive viewing experience, interactive tours empower buyers to take control of their exploration, guiding their journey through the property at their own pace and direction. With the click of a button or the swipe of a finger, buyers can zoom in on details, rotate their viewpoint, and navigate seamlessly from room to room, gaining a comprehensive understanding of the property's layout and design.

Moreover, interactive tours offer a level of accessibility and convenience that traditional property viewings simply cannot match. Prospective buyers no longer need to schedule appointments or travel to physical locations; instead, they can explore properties from the comfort of their own homes, at any time of day or night. This accessibility not only saves buyers time and effort but also opens up new opportunities for reaching and engaging with a broader audience of potential buyers.

The capacity of interactive property tours to create strong emotional bonds between purchasers and properties, however, may be their greatest benefit. Interactive tours help purchasers develop a stronger emotional connection to a home by immersing them in the virtual area of the property and enabling them to picture themselves living there, imagine the potential for the future, and imagine living there. Buyers may find that this emotional connection is a strong incentive to move on with the purchase of the property.

For real estate professionals, interactive property tours represent a game-changing tool for marketing and sales. By offering immersive, interactive experiences to prospective buyers, agents can differentiate their listings from the competition, attract more qualified leads, and ultimately close sales faster. Moreover, interactive tours provide agents with valuable insights into buyer preferences and behavior, enabling them to tailor their marketing strategies and offerings to better meet the needs of their clients.

As we continue to embrace the digital transformation of the real estate industry, interactive property tours stand at the forefront of innovation, offering unparalleled opportunities for engaging buyers and driving sales. Whether you're a buyer searching for your dream home or a seller looking to showcase your property in the best possible light, interactive tours offer a glimpse into the future of real estate—a future where immersive experiences reign supreme, and the possibilities are endless.

Virtual Staging

In the dynamic landscape of real estate marketing, the concept of virtual staging has emerged as a game-changing innovation, revolutionizing the way empty properties are presented to prospective buyers. Virtual staging harnesses the power of technology to transform vacant spaces into inviting, fully-furnished homes, enhancing their appeal and maximizing their potential in the eyes of buyers.

At its core, virtual staging is the art of digitally furnishing and decorating empty spaces to create immersive visualizations of what a property could look like when furnished. Through the use of advanced rendering software and digital design techniques, virtual stagers can add furniture, decor, and even architectural elements to vacant rooms, bringing them to life in vivid detail.

One of the primary benefits of virtual staging is its ability to help buyers visualize the possibilities of a space. Unlike traditional staging, which relies on physical furniture and decor, virtual staging offers unlimited flexibility and customization options. From contemporary chic to rustic charm, virtual stagers can tailor their designs to suit the preferences and tastes of target buyers, creating immersive visualizations that resonate with their desires and aspirations.

Moreover, virtual staging allows for rapid experimentation and iteration, enabling sellers to showcase multiple design concepts and layouts without the time and expense of physically moving furniture. This flexibility not only accelerates the marketing process but also empowers sellers to adapt their staging strategies to changing market trends and buyer preferences, ensuring that their properties always make a strong impression.

But perhaps the most significant advantage of virtual staging is its cost-effectiveness. Traditional staging can be prohibitively expensive, requiring sellers to invest significant sums of money in renting furniture, hiring movers, and paying professional stagers. In contrast, virtual staging offers a more affordable alternative, with prices typically ranging from a fraction of the cost of traditional staging. This cost savings not only benefits sellers but also enables real estate agents to offer virtual staging as a value-added service to their clients, further enhancing their marketing efforts and distinguishing their listings from the competition.

Furthermore, virtual staging is not limited by geographical constraints or logistical challenges. Whether the property is located in a bustling urban center or a remote rural area, virtual stagers can work their magic from anywhere in the world, delivering stunning visualizations that captivate buyers and drive interest in the property.

As we continue to navigate the ever-evolving landscape of real estate marketing, virtual staging stands as a powerful tool for transforming empty spaces into desirable homes. Whether you're a seller looking to showcase your property in the best possible light or a buyer searching for your dream home, virtual staging offers a glimpse into the endless possibilities of what a space could become—a vision of comfort, style, and endless potential.

Remote Collaboration Tools: Streamlining Communication and Decision Making

In an increasingly interconnected world, where distance no longer dictates the limits of our interactions, remote collaboration tools have emerged as indispensable assets in the realm of real estate. These innovative technologies break down barriers, facilitating seamless communication and decision-making processes among stakeholders, regardless of their geographical locations.

At the core of remote collaboration tools lies the ability to connect individuals in real time, fostering collaboration and synergy among team members spread across different locations. Through the use of video conferencing, instant messaging, and virtual meeting platforms, real estate professionals can communicate effortlessly, sharing ideas, updates, and feedback with colleagues, clients, and partners with just a few clicks.

One of the primary advantages of remote collaboration tools is their ability to streamline communication, eliminating the delays and inefficiencies associated with traditional modes of communication such as phone calls and emails. With remote collaboration tools, important information can be shared instantaneously, enabling teams to stay aligned and informed in real time, even when working from different time zones or continents.

Moreover, remote collaboration tools empower stakeholders to make informed decisions more efficiently by providing access to relevant data and resources whenever and wherever they are needed. From accessing property listings and market reports to reviewing design plans and financial documents, remote collaboration tools ensure that decision-makers have the information they need at their fingertips, enabling them to make timely, well-informed choices that drive the success of their projects.

But perhaps the most significant advantage of remote collaboration tools is their ability to foster a sense of connection and cohesion among team members, even when they are physically separated. By facilitating face-to-face interactions through video conferencing and virtual meetings, remote collaboration tools help build trust, rapport, and camaraderie among colleagues, enhancing teamwork and collaboration in ways that transcend geographical boundaries.

Furthermore, remote collaboration tools offer flexibility and scalability, allowing teams to adapt and evolve in response to changing needs and circumstances. Whether collaborating on a small-scale project or managing a large-scale development, remote collaboration tools provide the scalability and versatility to meet the unique requirements of any endeavor, enabling teams to work smarter, faster, and more effectively.

Remote collaboration solutions are quite helpful as we traverse the complexity of today's real estate market. They enable teams to overcome geographical obstacles and achieve success by facilitating smooth communication and decision-making. Using remote collaboration solutions can open up new options, boost productivity, and take your projects to new heights of success whether you're an investor, developer, or real estate agent.

Blockchain in Real Estate Transactions

In the fast-paced world of real estate transactions, where trust and transparency are paramount, blockchain technology has emerged as a groundbreaking force, promising to revolutionize the way properties are bought, sold, and managed. By providing a secure, decentralized ledger of transactions, blockchain technology offers unparalleled transparency, security, and efficiency, transforming the real estate industry as we know it.

At its core, blockchain is a distributed database that records transactions in a secure and immutable manner. Unlike traditional centralized databases, which are prone to manipulation and fraud, blockchain relies on cryptographic algorithms and consensus mechanisms to ensure that data remains tamper-proof and verifiable. This inherent transparency and security make blockchain an ideal solution for real estate transactions, where large sums of money and sensitive information are at stake.

One of the primary benefits of blockchain in real estate transactions is its ability to provide transparency throughout the entire transaction process. By recording every step of the transaction on a public ledger that is accessible to all parties involved, blockchain ensures that each party has a clear and unambiguous record of the transaction history, reducing the risk of disputes and misunderstandings.

Additionally, blockchain improves security by dispersing transaction data across a network of computers and encrypting it, making it nearly hard for unauthorized parties to access or change the data. This degree of protection not only safeguards private data like contracts, financial records, and property titles, but it also gives buyers, sellers, and investors peace of mind, which promotes credibility and trust in the real estate industry.

However, the ability of blockchain to automate and streamline the transaction process, lowering costs and inefficiencies connected with conventional techniques, may be the most revolutionary feature of blockchain in real estate transactions. Blockchain allows parties to automate various aspects of the transaction process, including escrow payments, title transfers, and property management tasks. This eliminates the need for middlemen and expedites the closing date. Smart contracts are self-executing contracts with the terms of the agreement directly written into code.

Furthermore, blockchain technology offers the potential to unlock new opportunities for fractional ownership and real estate investment, allowing individuals to invest in properties with greater ease and liquidity. Through the use of tokenization—a process by which real-world assets are represented digitally as tokens on a blockchain—investors can buy and sell fractions of properties, opening up real estate investment opportunities to a broader audience and democratizing access to the market.

As we embrace the transformative power of blockchain in real estate transactions, we stand on the brink of a new era of transparency, security, and efficiency in the industry. Whether you're a buyer, seller, investor, or real estate professional, blockchain technology offers the promise of a more transparent, secure, and accessible real estate market—one where transactions are conducted with confidence, trust, and efficiency.

AI-Powered Property Insights: Leveraging Data Analytics for Informed Decisions

Artificial intelligence (AI) has emerged as a potent ally in the dynamic real estate market, where data is king. AI enables stakeholders to get deeper insights and make more educated decisions. Artificial intelligence (AI)-powered property insights provide a revolutionary method for comprehending market trends, projecting property prices, and spotting investment opportunities. They do this by utilizing sophisticated data analytics and machine learning algorithms.

At the heart of AI-powered property insights lies the ability to analyze vast amounts of data with speed and precision, uncovering patterns and correlations that may not be immediately apparent to human analysts. By leveraging machine learning algorithms, AI can sift through terabytes of real estate data—from property listings and transaction histories to demographic trends and economic indicators—and extract actionable insights that drive strategic decision-making.

One of the primary benefits of AI-powered property insights is their ability to provide real-time, data-driven analysis of market conditions and property valuations. Unlike traditional methods of market analysis, which rely on historical data and manual analysis, AI algorithms can process large volumes of data in real time, enabling stakeholders to quickly assess market trends, identify emerging opportunities, and make informed decisions with confidence.

Moreover, AI-powered property insights offer unparalleled accuracy and reliability, thanks to their ability to detect subtle patterns and trends that may go unnoticed by human analysts. By analyzing data from diverse sources and applying sophisticated statistical models, AI algorithms can provide more accurate property valuations, forecast market trends, and identify potential risks and opportunities with greater precision, minimizing the potential for costly errors and missed opportunities.

But perhaps the most transformative aspect of AI-powered property insights is their ability to personalize and customize recommendations based on individual preferences and objectives. Through the use of predictive analytics and recommendation engines, AI algorithms can tailor their insights to the unique needs and goals of each stakeholder, providing personalized recommendations for property investments, financing options, and strategic decisions.

Furthermore, AI-powered property insights offer scalability and versatility, enabling stakeholders to analyze data across diverse markets, property types, and investment strategies. Whether analyzing residential properties, commercial real estate, or investment portfolios, AI algorithms can adapt to the specific requirements of each scenario, providing valuable insights and recommendations that drive success in any context.

We are at the cusp of a new era in real estate decision-making as we embrace the transformative potential of AI-powered property analytics. AI technology holds the potential to provide deeper insights, better judgments, and greater success in the fast-paced and cutthroat real estate market, regardless of your role in the transaction—as a buyer, seller, investor, or real estate professional.

Smart Home Integration

In the era of rapid technological advancement, the concept of smart home integration has emerged as a beacon of innovation, reshaping the way we interact with and experience our living spaces. By seamlessly integrating cutting-edge technology into the fabric of our homes, smart home systems offer unparalleled convenience, comfort, and sustainability, ushering in a new era of connected living.

At its core, smart home integration involves the incorporation of Internet of Things (IoT) devices and automation systems into residential properties, enabling homeowners to control and monitor various aspects of their homes remotely through smartphones, tablets, or voice commands. From lighting and heating to security and entertainment, smart home systems provide a centralized platform for managing and optimizing the functionality of our living spaces.

One of the primary benefits of smart home integration is its ability to enhance convenience and efficiency in our daily lives. Through the use of IoT devices such as smart thermostats, lighting controls, and automated appliances, homeowners can automate routine tasks, adjust settings remotely, and optimize energy usage, saving time, money, and resources in the process.

Moreover, smart home integration offers a heightened level of comfort and customization, allowing homeowners to tailor their living environments to suit their preferences and lifestyles. Whether dimming the lights for a cozy movie night, adjusting the thermostat for optimal comfort, or setting the perfect ambiance with customized lighting scenes, smart home systems empower homeowners to create personalized living spaces that reflect their individual tastes and needs.

But perhaps the most transformative aspect of smart home integration is its potential to promote sustainability and environmental responsibility. By monitoring energy usage, optimizing resource consumption, and promoting eco-friendly practices, smart home systems enable homeowners to reduce their carbon footprint and contribute to a more sustainable future.

Through the use of energy-efficient appliances, smart lighting controls, and renewable energy sources such as solar panels and geothermal heating systems, smart homes can significantly reduce energy consumption and greenhouse gas emissions, helping to mitigate the impact of climate change and preserve our planet for future generations.

Furthermore, smart home integration offers the potential to enhance safety and security in our living spaces. Through the use of connected surveillance cameras, smart locks, and motion sensors, homeowners can monitor and protect their homes from potential threats, receiving instant alerts and notifications in the event of suspicious activity or emergencies.

As we embrace the transformative power of smart home integration, we stand on the brink of a new era of connected, sustainable living. Whether you're a homeowner looking to enhance comfort and convenience or a developer seeking to incorporate cutting-edge technology into your properties, smart home integration offers limitless possibilities for creating smarter, more efficient, and more sustainable living spaces that enrich our lives and our planet.

Digital Marketing Strategies

In the fast-paced world of real estate marketing, where digital channels reign supreme, the ability to captivate and engage audiences in a virtual environment has become essential for success. With the rise of online platforms and social media, digital marketing strategies offer unparalleled opportunities to reach and connect with potential buyers in ways that were once unimaginable. By harnessing the power of technology and creativity, real estate professionals can leverage digital marketing strategies to build brand awareness, drive leads, and ultimately close sales in today's virtual landscape.

At the core of digital marketing strategies lies the ability to create compelling and immersive experiences that resonate with audiences on a personal level. Whether through captivating video content, interactive virtual tours, or engaging social media campaigns, digital marketing allows real estate professionals to tell stories, evoke emotions, and establish meaningful connections with their target audience.

One of the primary benefits of digital marketing strategies is their ability to reach a wider audience than traditional marketing methods. Through the use of online platforms such as websites, social media, and search engines, real estate professionals can extend their reach beyond geographic boundaries, targeting potential buyers wherever they may be and engaging with them in real time.

Moreover, digital marketing strategies offer unparalleled flexibility and versatility, enabling real estate professionals to tailor their messaging and content to suit the preferences and interests of their target audience. Whether promoting a luxury waterfront property or a cozy suburban home, digital marketing allows for highly targeted and personalized campaigns that resonate with specific demographics and segments.

But perhaps the most transformative aspect of digital marketing strategies is their ability to track and measure results in real time, providing valuable insights into audience behavior and preferences. Through the use of analytics tools and data tracking technologies, real estate professionals can monitor the performance of their campaigns, identify areas for improvement, and optimize their strategies for maximum impact.

Furthermore, digital marketing strategies offer the potential to foster engagement and interaction with audiences in ways that traditional marketing methods simply cannot match. Whether through live virtual events, interactive webinars, or immersive virtual reality experiences, digital marketing allows real estate professionals to create memorable and meaningful interactions with their audience, driving engagement, loyalty, and ultimately, conversions.

As we navigate the ever-changing landscape of real estate marketing, digital marketing strategies stand as powerful tools for engaging audiences in a virtual environment. Whether you're a real estate agent, developer, or marketer, embracing digital marketing offers limitless opportunities to connect with your audience, tell your story, and drive success in today's digital-first world.

Online Auction Platforms: Modernizing Property Sales Processes

The advent of online auction platforms has brought about a paradigm change in the ever-changing real estate market, transforming the conventional property sales process and creating new avenues for buyers, sellers, and investors. Online auction platforms, which are revolutionizing the way transactions are carried out in today's digital landscape, offer a simplified, transparent, and effective approach to buy and sell assets by utilizing technology and innovation.

At the heart of online auction platforms lies the ability to create a competitive and transparent marketplace where buyers can bid on properties in real time from the comfort of their own homes. Unlike traditional auctions, which require physical attendance and are often limited by geographic constraints, online auctions offer a level playing field for buyers from around the world, enabling them to participate in auctions regardless of their location.

One of the primary benefits of online auction platforms is their ability to streamline the sales process, reducing the time and effort required to sell a property. By providing a centralized platform for listing properties, conducting auctions, and facilitating transactions, online auction platforms eliminate the need for time-consuming negotiations, paperwork, and logistics, enabling properties to be sold quickly and efficiently.

Moreover, online auction platforms offer unparalleled transparency and visibility into the sales process, providing buyers and sellers with real-time access to information about bidding activity, property details, and transaction status. Through the use of advanced technology and data analytics, online auction platforms enable stakeholders to make informed decisions based on accurate and up-to-date information, fostering trust and confidence in the marketplace.

But perhaps the most transformative aspect of online auction platforms is their ability to create a competitive bidding environment that drives property values and maximizes returns for sellers. By attracting a larger pool of potential buyers and encouraging competitive bidding, online auctions often result in higher sale prices and faster transactions than traditional sales methods, benefiting both sellers and buyers alike.

Additionally, online auction platforms allow vendors and buyers to engage in auctions at any time and from any location, giving them both flexibility and convenience. Online auction platforms offer a practical and effective way to trade in today's fast-paced real estate market, whether you're buying a vacation house, selling an investment property, or liquidating a portfolio of assets.

We are on the verge of a new era in real estate transactions as we embrace the revolutionary potential of online auction platforms. This new age will see creativity and technology coming together to create a more accessible, transparent, and efficient marketplace for buyers and sellers. Online auction platforms provide countless chances to purchase, sell, and invest in real estate with ease and confidence, regardless of your level of experience or expertise in real estate.

Virtual Property Management

In the ever-evolving landscape of property management, the concept of virtual property management has emerged as a transformative force, leveraging technology to streamline the monitoring and maintenance of properties in the digital realm. By harnessing the power of data analytics, remote monitoring systems, and automation tools, virtual property management offers unprecedented efficiency, convenience, and scalability for property owners, managers, and tenants alike.

At its core, virtual property management involves the use of digital tools and platforms to monitor, analyze, and optimize the performance of properties remotely. From tracking energy usage and maintenance requests to managing security systems and tenant communications, virtual property management systems provide a centralized platform for overseeing all aspects of property operations from anywhere in the world.

One of the primary benefits of virtual property management is its ability to enhance efficiency and reduce costs by automating routine tasks and streamlining workflows. Through the use of IoT devices, sensors, and smart systems, virtual property management platforms can collect real-time data about various aspects of property performance, such as energy consumption, equipment status, and occupancy levels, enabling proactive maintenance and optimization strategies that minimize downtime and maximize efficiency.

Moreover, virtual property management offers unparalleled transparency and visibility into property operations, providing owners and managers with real-time access to data and insights about property performance and tenant behavior. By analyzing this data, property managers can identify trends, patterns, and opportunities for improvement, enabling them to make data-driven decisions that enhance the overall value and profitability of their properties.

But perhaps the most transformative aspect of virtual property management is its ability to improve tenant satisfaction and retention by providing a more seamless and responsive experience. Through the use of digital communication channels, tenants can submit maintenance requests, pay rent, and communicate with property managers in real time, eliminating the need for time-consuming phone calls or emails and ensuring that issues are addressed promptly and efficiently.

Furthermore, virtual property management offers scalability and flexibility, enabling property owners and managers to oversee multiple properties from a single dashboard and adapt to changing needs and circumstances with ease.

Whether managing a single-family home, a multi-unit apartment building, or a commercial office space, virtual property management systems provide the tools and resources needed to optimize property performance and deliver exceptional service to tenants.

As we embrace the transformative potential of virtual property management, we stand on the brink of a new era of property operations, one where technology and innovation converge to create more efficient, responsive, and sustainable living and working environments. Whether you're a property owner, manager, or tenant, virtual property management offers limitless opportunities to optimize performance, enhance satisfaction, and unlock the full potential of your properties in the digital age.

Remote Work and the Future of Commercial Real Estate

In the wake of global shifts towards remote work, the commercial real estate landscape is undergoing a profound transformation, necessitating a reevaluation of how office spaces are designed, utilized, and valued. As businesses embrace flexible work arrangements and digital collaboration tools, the traditional office model is evolving to meet the changing needs and preferences of the modern workforce. The future of commercial real estate lies in adapting spaces to accommodate new work trends, fostering collaboration, creativity, and community while maximizing efficiency and flexibility.

At the heart of this transformation is the recognition that the physical office is no longer just a place to work but a hub for collaboration, connection, and culture. As remote work becomes more prevalent, office spaces are evolving to prioritize amenities and features that promote collaboration, creativity, and employee well-being. From open-plan layouts and flexible workspaces to communal areas and wellness facilities, the office of the future is designed to inspire and engage employees, fostering a sense of belonging and community even in a remote-first world.

Moreover, the future of commercial real estate lies in embracing flexibility and adaptability, enabling tenants to scale their space and services to meet their evolving needs and priorities. With the rise of remote work and distributed teams, businesses are seeking flexible leasing arrangements that allow them to adjust their space requirements in real time, whether scaling up for growth or downsizing to reduce costs. Flexible lease terms, coworking spaces, and on-demand services are becoming increasingly popular options for businesses looking to adapt to changing work trends while minimizing risk and overhead.

The repurposing and redesigning of current office spaces to match new demands and expectations, however, may have the most impact on commercial real estate as a result of remote work. The office is becoming less of a typical workspace and more of a hub for invention, collaboration, and culture-building as companies embrace remote-first policies and hybrid work arrangements. With an emphasis on creating settings that inspire creativity, create collaboration, and promote a sense of belonging, office spaces are being renovated with flexibility, connection, and employee well-being as top priorities.

Furthermore, the future of commercial real estate lies in embracing technology and innovation to enhance the workplace experience and optimize space utilization. From smart building systems and IoT sensors to virtual reality tools and digital collaboration platforms, technology is playing an increasingly important role in shaping the future of office design and management. By leveraging data and analytics, businesses can gain insights into how their spaces are used, identify opportunities for optimization, and create more efficient and productive work environments.

As we navigate the evolving landscape of commercial real estate in the era of remote work, the key to success lies in embracing change, innovation, and collaboration. By adapting spaces to accommodate new work trends, fostering flexibility and connectivity, and prioritizing employee well-being and engagement, commercial real estate professionals can create spaces that not only meet the needs of today's workforce but also anticipate the demands of the future. The future of commercial real estate is bright, and by embracing change and embracing innovation, we can build a more resilient, flexible, and vibrant built environment for generations to come.

Cybersecurity Measures

In an increasingly digital world, where information is one of the most valuable assets, cybersecurity has become a paramount concern for businesses operating in the real estate industry. With the rise of online transactions, cloud-based systems, and remote work, the risk of cyber threats such as data breaches, ransomware attacks, and identity theft has never been greater. As custodians of sensitive client information and valuable digital assets, real estate professionals must prioritize cybersecurity measures to safeguard their data, protect their clients, and maintain the trust and integrity of their businesses.

At the forefront of cybersecurity measures is the implementation of robust data protection protocols to safeguard sensitive information from unauthorized access, manipulation, or theft. This includes encrypting data both in transit and at rest, implementing multi-factor authentication for access to critical systems, and regularly updating security software and firewalls to defend against emerging threats.

Cybersecurity measures involve educating employees and clients about best practices for data security and privacy. This includes providing training on recognizing phishing attempts, avoiding malware-infected websites, and using secure password practices to prevent unauthorized access to accounts and systems. By fostering a culture of cybersecurity awareness and vigilance, real estate professionals can empower their teams and clients to protect themselves from cyber threats and minimize the risk of data breaches.

But perhaps the most critical aspect of cybersecurity measures is the establishment of robust incident response and recovery plans to mitigate the impact of cyber-attacks and ensure business continuity in the event of a breach. This includes regularly backing up data to secure offsite locations, maintaining disaster recovery and incident response protocols, and establishing clear communication channels for reporting and responding to security incidents in a timely and effective manner.

Furthermore, cybersecurity measures involve staying abreast of the latest threats and trends in cybersecurity and adapting security measures accordingly. This includes monitoring industry news and updates, participating in cybersecurity training and certification programs, and collaborating with cybersecurity experts and industry peers to share insights and best practices for mitigating cyber risks.

The secret to success in navigating the intricate and always changing world of cybersecurity in the real estate industry is to protect digital assets and client data in a proactive and thorough manner. Real estate professionals can protect their businesses and keep their clients' trust in an increasingly digital world by putting strong data protection protocols in place, teaching staff and clients about cybersecurity best practices, creating incident response and recovery plans, and keeping up with emerging trends and threats.

Proptech Investments: Opportunities and Challenges in Tech-Driven Ventures

In the realm of real estate, the convergence of technology and innovation has given rise to a burgeoning sector known as "proptech," which encompasses a wide range of tech-driven ventures aimed at revolutionizing various aspects of the industry. From property management and brokerage to construction and development, proptech startups are leveraging cutting-edge technologies such as artificial intelligence, blockchain, and virtual reality to disrupt traditional business models and unlock new opportunities for growth and innovation.

At the heart of proptech investments lie the immense opportunities for unlocking value and driving efficiencies across the real estate value chain. By harnessing technology to streamline processes, automate tasks, and improve decision-making, proptech startups offer the potential to reduce costs, increase operational efficiency, and enhance the overall customer experience for stakeholders across the industry.

One of the primary opportunities presented by proptech investments is the potential to address longstanding pain points and inefficiencies in the real estate industry. Whether streamlining property transactions, optimizing building operations, or improving tenant engagement, proptech startups are pioneering innovative solutions to complex challenges, offering tangible benefits for property owners, managers, investors, and occupants alike.

Moreover, proptech investments offer the potential for significant returns for investors willing to embrace innovation and disruption. As the demand for tech-driven solutions continues to grow, proptech startups have attracted substantial investment from venture capital firms, private equity investors, and corporate players looking to capitalize on the transformative power of technology in real estate.

But alongside the opportunities, proptech investments also pose unique challenges and risks that must be carefully navigated. One of the key challenges facing proptech startups is the need to navigate regulatory complexities and industry standards, which vary significantly across different markets and jurisdictions. From compliance with data privacy regulations to navigating zoning laws and building codes, proptech startups must demonstrate a deep understanding of regulatory requirements and industry best practices to succeed in the highly regulated real estate industry.

Furthermore, proptech investments face challenges related to market acceptance and adoption, as traditional players may be resistant to change or slow to embrace new technologies. Overcoming inertia and convincing stakeholders to adopt innovative solutions often requires education, collaboration, and a strong value proposition that clearly demonstrates the benefits of proptech solutions in improving efficiency, reducing costs, and enhancing the overall value proposition for stakeholders.

As we navigate the opportunities and challenges of proptech investments, the key to success lies in fostering collaboration, innovation, and entrepreneurship across the real estate ecosystem. By investing in technology-driven ventures that address real-world problems, embrace regulatory compliance, and demonstrate a clear value proposition for stakeholders, investors can unlock new opportunities for growth and innovation in the dynamic and ever-evolving world of real estate.

The Next Frontier

As the real estate industry continues its evolution into the digital age, the next frontier lies in anticipating emerging technologies and trends that will shape the future of virtual ventures in the sector. From virtual reality and artificial intelligence to blockchain and decentralized finance, the possibilities for innovation are endless, offering new opportunities for stakeholders to reimagine how properties are bought, sold, managed, and experienced in the virtual realm.

At the forefront of this exploration is virtual reality (VR), which promises to revolutionize property exploration and visualization in ways never before imagined. By creating immersive, interactive experiences that allow users to explore properties from anywhere in the world, VR technology offers a powerful tool for engaging buyers, showcasing properties, and facilitating remote transactions.

From virtual property tours to immersive staging experiences, VR has the potential to transform the way we buy, sell, and experience real estate in the digital age.

Moreover, artificial intelligence (AI) is poised to play a central role in driving innovation and efficiency in virtual ventures in the real estate industry. By harnessing the power of machine learning algorithms and predictive analytics, AI can provide valuable insights into market trends, property valuations, and investment opportunities, empowering stakeholders to make informed decisions with confidence. From AI-powered property insights to smart home automation systems, AI technology offers endless possibilities for enhancing the efficiency, convenience, and sustainability of virtual ventures in real estate.

But perhaps the most transformative technology on the horizon is blockchain, which promises to revolutionize the way real estate transactions are conducted, recorded, and verified. By providing a secure, transparent, and decentralized ledger of property ownership and transactions, blockchain technology offers unparalleled transparency, security, and efficiency, reducing the risk of fraud, streamlining processes, and unlocking new opportunities for investment and financing in the real estate market.

Furthermore, the emergence of decentralized finance (DeFi) presents exciting new possibilities for virtual ventures in real estate, enabling stakeholders to access liquidity, invest in properties, and participate in crowdfunding and fractional ownership models without the need for traditional intermediaries. By leveraging blockchain technology and smart contracts, DeFi platforms offer a decentralized and transparent alternative to traditional financing and investment models, democratizing access to the real estate market and unlocking new opportunities for growth and innovation.

As we look to the future of virtual ventures in the real estate industry, the possibilities are endless. By embracing emerging technologies such as virtual reality, artificial intelligence, blockchain, and decentralized finance, stakeholders can unlock new opportunities for innovation, efficiency, and sustainability in the dynamic and ever-evolving world of real estate. The next frontier awaits, and by anticipating emerging technologies and trends, we can chart a course towards a more connected, transparent, and inclusive future for virtual ventures in real estate.

Conclusion

In the journey through the pages of "Virtual Ventures: Exploring Tech Trends in the Real Estate Industry," we have embarked on a captivating exploration of the transformative power of technology and innovation in reshaping the landscape of real estate. From virtual reality and artificial intelligence to blockchain and decentralized finance, the possibilities for innovation and disruption are limitless, offering new opportunities for growth, efficiency, and sustainability in the digital age.

As we reflect on the insights shared within these chapters, it becomes evident that the future of real estate lies in embracing emerging technologies and trends that redefine how properties are bought, sold, managed, and experienced. Whether through immersive virtual property tours, AI-powered property insights, or blockchain-enabled transactions, the potential for innovation is vast, offering new ways to engage buyers, optimize operations, and unlock value in the real estate market.

Moreover, the journey through "Virtual Ventures" has highlighted the importance of collaboration, innovation, and adaptability in navigating the complexities of the digital landscape. In a world where change is constant and disruption is the norm, success in the real estate industry requires a willingness to embrace new ideas, experiment with new technologies, and evolve with the shifting needs and expectations of clients, tenants, and investors.

As we stand on the brink of a new era of real estate innovation, the lessons learned from "Virtual Ventures" serve as a guide for navigating the challenges and opportunities that lie ahead. By embracing emerging technologies, fostering collaboration, and staying ahead of the curve, real estate professionals can unlock new opportunities for growth and innovation, driving success in the dynamic and ever-evolving world of real estate in the digital age.

In closing, "Virtual Ventures" invites readers to embrace the future of real estate with optimism, curiosity, and a spirit of innovation. As we embark on this journey together, let us seize the opportunities that lie ahead, charting a course towards a more connected, transparent, and sustainable future for real estate in the digital age.